8
5
3
7
5
4
1
9
8
1
9
3
5
2
1
6
4
7
5
3

THE LITTLE BOOK OF
NUMEROLOGY

ELSIE WILD

summersdale

THE LITTLE BOOK OF NUMEROLOGY

Cover images and chapter pages © Luxcor/Shutterstock.com
Lines and circles on p.9 and throughout © Gigi Pattern/Shutterstock.com

Text by Ellen Ricks

An Hachette UK Company
www.hachette.co.uk

Summersdale Publishers Ltd
Part of Octopus Publishing Group Limited
Carmelite House
50 Victoria Embankment
LONDON
EC4Y 0DZ
UK

www.summersdale.com

Printed and bound in China

ISBN: 978-1-80007-449-1

Substantial discounts on bulk quantities of Summersdale books are available to corporations, professional associations and other organizations. For details contact general enquiries: telephone: +44 (0) 1243 771107 or email: enquiries@summersdale.com.

★ CONTENTS ★

★ DISCLAIMER ★

The author and the publisher cannot accept responsibility for any misuse or misunderstanding of any information contained herein, or any loss, damage or injury, be it health, financial or otherwise, suffered by any individual or group acting upon or relying on information contained herein.

⋆ INTRODUCTION ⋆

Numbers affect every part of our lives; what time to go to bed, how much money we have, how old we are. But what if we told you that numbers have a bigger, more magical purpose? That seeing 11.11 on the clock tells us more than what the time is? That seeing the number 33.33 on your receipt isn't a coincidence? That the date on which you were born was handpicked by the universe and influences your destiny?

That is the magic of numerology. It can show you who you are and who you can become. It can also bring you secret messages from the universe. While this knowledge can be intimidating, cracking the code isn't hard. You don't need to be a mathematician to figure it out. If you have a calculator, you have everything you need to unlock the secrets of numerology. This book will guide you through all areas of this mystical practice, from charts to divination, making it as easy as 1, 2, 3.

So, let's get started.

CHAPTER ONE:

WHAT IS NUMEROLOGY?

Numerology studies the magical connection between numbers and their influence on our world. Numerology is based on the belief that single-digit numbers have a special vibration and unique meanings that guide and influence our lives. The date of your birth can reveal insight into your personality and destiny. A repeating number or number sequence can indicate a hidden message from the universe. Even the letters in names have a numerical value that we can study and gain insight into. When we understand the secret language of numbers, we can start to crack the code within ourselves and the wider world.

★ NUMBER VIBRATIONS ★

All numbers can be calculated into a single-digit number from one to nine. In numerology, these single figures have unique symbolic meanings called vibrations. Whether you want to find the special meaning behind your birth date or pick when to have your wedding, you can determine the vibrations of that date by adding it up to a single-digit number.

Here's a quick overview of the vibrations associated with each number:

1: Leadership, independence, uniqueness, action.
2: Partnerships, balance, intuition, emotions.
3: Creativity, optimism, inspiration, communication.
4: Hard work, organization, practicality, service.
5: Freedom, curiosity, experience, change.
6: Family, responsibility, protection, care.
7: Introspection, spirituality, solitude, study.
8: Success, authority, karma, power.
9: Compassion, enlightenment, generosity, completion.

Keep these numbers and meanings in mind as you go through this book and your life!

✦ WHAT ABOUT ZERO? ✦

As you may have noticed, the number zero hasn't been mentioned. Zero doesn't have its own vibration. It doesn't bring anything when added to another number or take anything away when subtracted. It simply reflects the other number. For example, 2+0 is still 2, and 3-0 is still 3. Because it doesn't have a unique vibration, zero doesn't have its own significance in numerology. If you happen to run across a zero – whether adding up your numerology profile or in a sequence of numbers – know that it heightens the numbers surrounding it. For example, the number 20 will amplify the 2's energy. The more zeros you see, the more amplified the other numbers (which is why you like to see them in your bank account), as long as another number goes with it.

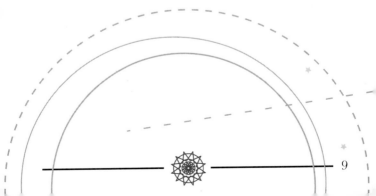

✦ MASTER NUMBERS ✦

While adding all numbers together can form a single digit, three numbers are considered more powerful as a pair – when these numbers double, the vibrations become supercharged, making them special. Such numbers are known as master numbers. Master numbers are two-digit numbers that amplify the power and potential of the number in their pairing. Only 11, 22 and 33 are considered master numbers: they represent what is known as the Triangle of Enlightenment.

Master numbers hold great power and influence; it's why numerologists make wishes when the clock strikes 11.11. However, this power can also bring challenges. You don't become a "master" at something without learning a few hard lessons, and master numbers can initiate trials in your life to help you learn and grow. This situation is especially true if your life path number is a master number, which we'll explore further in Chapter Three (page 28).

Here is a quick overview of the master numbers:

11 – THE VISIONARY

The most intuitive of all the master numbers, 11 represents the connection to our subconscious mind. Seeing 11 can mean that you are encouraged to look beyond the limitations of the physical realm and ask what you can do differently. This master number represents higher ideals, invention and faith and motivates us to find equilibrium in all areas of life, from work and play to finding balance in our mind, body and spirit.

22 – THE CREATOR

The number 22 represents turning dreams into reality, as well as duality, responsibility and the work ethic to accomplish great things. However, in our attempts to build something that lasts, we will most likely fail – a lot. Seeing 22 should encourage us to not fear failure. Instead, we should embrace the possibility that we can achieve great things with effort.

33 – THE DELIVERER

The rarest of the three master numbers, 33 acts as our spiritual teacher by guiding us through life's many ups and downs. This number represents energy, passion and unconditional love and seeks to support humanity by bringing more joy and passion and seeking out the world's secrets. 33 demonstrates that you can go through the darkest times and come back stronger and kinder than ever.

Of all the metaphysical practices, numerology is one of the easiest to learn and has uses throughout your life, from self-analysis to divination. Once you understand the basics, you can do quite a few things with this knowledge.

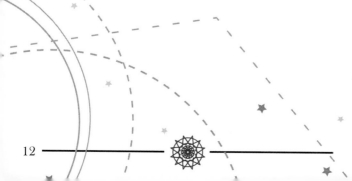

✶ ANALYZING DATES ✶

If you have a big event coming up, such as an important presentation or even your wedding, then numerology can help determine how that day might unfold. By breaking down the date into a single-digit number, you can understand the day's vibration and plan accordingly.

For example, if the date is the fourth of the month, it will involve hard work and dealing with your responsibilities (as per the vibrations listed on page 8). However, if you're looking to plan an event such as a wedding, look for dates that equal more romantic numbers: 2, 3, 6 or 9.

Numerology can even predict what kind of year you will have. Each person has a personal year likely to give them the lessons, challenges and gifts required to proceed to the next phase of life. There will be more information on that later.

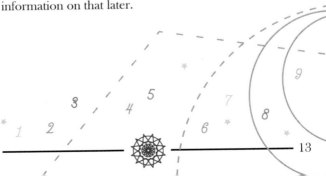

NUMBERS ARE THE HIGHEST DEGREE OF KNOWLEDGE. IT IS KNOWLEDGE ITSELF.

PLATO

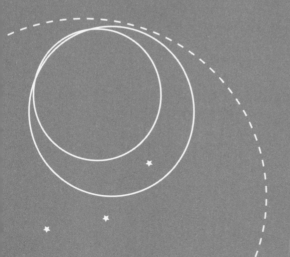

✦ NUMEROLOGY TOOLS ✦

Numerology is one of the simplest metaphysical practices because you do not need much equipment. The calculations used in numerology only require basic arithmetic, so, at most, you'll need a calculator. However, if you don't have one of those, you can use a piece of paper and a pencil, or even your fingers and toes. So, breathe a sigh of relief and put your protractor away.

However, the most valuable tool you'll use in this book isn't a calculator, but an open mind. For numerology to really work, you must remain open to the possibility that numbers have more than just monetary value. You must believe that they carry energy and vibrations that can affect and enchant your life. This book can teach you the basics but cannot impact your life if you are unwilling to entertain the thought.

If you are open to the possibility of the power of numbers, then welcome to the magic of numerology.

CHAPTER TWO:

A BRIEF HISTORY OF NUMEROLOGY

While numerical systems go back more than 40,000 years, it is thought that the act of counting pre-dates language. The ability to count forms part of human biology, so no wonder numbers hold so much significance in our lives. While the term "numerology" didn't appear in English until the early 1900s, numerology has existed for thousands of years, appearing in almost every ancient civilization, including Egypt, Babylon, China, Rome, India, Japan and Greece. To best understand modern numerology, we must look at the systems that came before it and the ones still practised today.

NUMEROLOGY ★ THROUGHOUT TIME ★

Numbers have had a huge impact on people and cultures across the world. Here is a breakdown of some of numerology's uses throughout history.

CHALDEAN NUMEROLOGY

One of the oldest forms of numerology, Chaldean numerology came to life in ancient Mesopotamia around 10 BCE. It is based on the idea that certain numbers emit specific vibrations that carry meaning. Like astrology, also discovered in Mesopotamia, Chaldean numerology was used to make predictions. Like modern numerology, Chaldean numerology takes the vibrations from your full name and birthday to predict your destiny. However, instead of using the numbers 1–9, the Chaldean numerology chart only goes up to 8. Nine is left out because its connection to infinity makes it one of the most sacred numbers.

KABBALAH NUMEROLOGY

Originating from Hebrew, Kabbalah numerology uses a particular form of the Hebrew alphabet to assign a numerical value to a name, word or phrase in a practice known as gematria. Recordings date gematria back to the tenth century BCE in Assyria, an ancient kingdom of Mesopotamia, in the form of an inscription commissioned by Sargon II, the king of the Neo-Assyrian Empire. The inscription stated that, "The king built the wall of Khorsabad 16,283 cubits long to correspond with the numerical value of his name."

Gematria and Kabbalah numerology focus more on name numerology than your actual birth date. By using Kabbalah numerology, you can connect with your inner source of power and align with your soul's purpose to guide you through life. It can also help increase your intuition and elevate your higher consciousness.

Kabbalah has seen a surge in popularity in recent years, thanks in part to celebrities such as Lucy Liu, Ashton Kutcher and Madonna taking an interest in the spiritual science.

PYTHAGOREAN NUMEROLOGY

This is the numerology that people are most familiar with. Greek philosopher and mathematician Pythagoras "discovered" this type of numerology in the sixth century BCE. You may remember this name from your maths, history or philosophy classes, but among all his great achievements, Pythagoras has become known as the father of modern numerology.

Numbers fascinated Pythagoras throughout his life, so much so that he travelled to Egypt to study Chaldean numerology. He believed that everything could translate into a single-digit number. This numerical system, similar to gematria, became known as the Pythagorean number system, which we will learn more about in Chapter Three.

Pythagorean numerology can predict events or someone's fate by applying the system to their name and date of birth. However, this type of numerology also holds that we have the power to alter our destiny by changing our names if we wish.

TAMIL NUMEROLOGY

Originating in the southern part of India in Tamil Nadu, Tamil numerology (sometimes known as Indian numerology) is similar to the Chaldean practice in that it uses your names and date of birth to calculate personal numbers. While a modern numerology profile (see page 30) has six digits, Tamil numerology has three:

- **Psychic Number:** The number that comes from adding the month and date of your birth.
- **Destiny Number:** The number that comes from adding the numbers in your date of birth, including the year.
- **Name Number:** The number that comes from adding the letters in your name, including your first name, middle name and surname.

Tamil numerology believes these numbers are attached to each and every person and can help us make sense of our reality. The relationship between these personal details and numbers holds information about our strengths, weaknesses and destiny.

CHINESE NUMEROLOGY

While many numerological systems focus on aspects of a person's destiny, Chinese numerology takes a more superstitious approach. It believes that some numbers are lucky while others may bring misfortune based on their vibrations. To this day, people will avoid certain numbers to prevent bad luck.

Here is a quick overview of what each number represents in Chinese numerology:

0: Represents beginnings and is considered lucky.

1: Neither lucky nor unlucky. One represents being single and can mean loneliness or being the "first" to achieve something.

2: Considered lucky as, according to Chinese beliefs, "all good things come in pairs".

3: Represents growth. Three is neither lucky nor unlucky, as growth can go in both directions, from growing into new stages of life to getting old or moving out of important phases.

4: Considered very unlucky, representing death. Like the unlucky number 13 in Western culture (which adds to 4), a major superstition in East Asia concerns the number 4, with hotels omitting it from their floors and room numbers.

5: Represents nothing, meaning it can be considered lucky or unlucky. However, the number 5 is associated with the elements of Taoism (water, fire, earth, wood and metal).

6: Represents profitability and happiness. It is considered a lucky number, especially in business.

7: Represents certainty. It can be either lucky or unlucky depending on the context, as being certain about something can be good or bad.

8: Considered the luckiest number in Chinese numerology and culture, the number 8 represents joy and prosperity. It is believed that numerous 8s can increase your luck, and people will try to use the number as often as possible.

9: Historically associated with the Emperor of China, the number 9 is often used in weddings to represent long-lasting relationships.

✦ NUMEROLOGY IN RELIGION ✦

While many religions look down on numerology and all forms of divination as immoral and satanic, numbers have appeared in every religion and often hold significant value. Here are a few examples.

3: There is the Holy Trinity of the Father, the Son and the Holy Spirit in the Catholic faith. In Wicca, there is the Maid, Mother and Crone, along with the Rule of Three (meaning the energy you put into the world will return to you three times over). In Kabbalah, the soul consists of three parts, and in Hinduism, there are three paths to salvation.

6: In the Book of Revelation, 666 is called the number of the beast and is associated with the devil.

7: There are seven sacraments in the Catholic faith. Christians believe in the seven deadly sins. There are also seven chakras.

8: There are eight nights of Hanukkah and eight Sabbats in Wicca, and 888 is known to represent Jesus (or, more specifically, Christ the Redeemer) and the number for infinite love.

★ FAMOUS USERS OF NUMEROLOGY ★

While Pythagoras is considered the father of numerology, others have used it to help create understanding and insight into their lives and careers.

SIR THOMAS BROWNE

An English polymath and author, Browne wrote *The Garden of Cyrus*, a discourse using numerology to explain that five appears throughout nature.

L. DOW BALLIETT

One of the most renowned numerologists of the 1800s, she helped bring numerology into public awareness and wrote some of the earliest books on its history. She helped modernize numerology for the twentieth century and talked about the vibrations of numbers.

DR CARL JUNG

Famed Swiss psychiatrist Dr Carl Jung was fascinated by numerology, believing that all numbers have a special meaning that can impact our unconscious mind. He thought it possible to tap into the messages the universe sent to us through numbers.

✶ NUMEROLOGY TODAY ✶

In today's world, numerology has become another popular form of divination and self-reflection, much like astrology and tarot. As more people discover their life path number, it can often act as a "lucky number" for them. For example, they may choose to include it in their clothing or accessories and use it when picking their lottery numbers. People even choose street addresses based on these numbers.

People also opt to use numerology in creative pursuits, incorporating vital numbers into their work. One example would be singer-songwriter Taylor Swift, who uses the number 13 (the day she was born) in her music, from the number of album tracks to release dates, based on if they add up to 13.

Now that we have learned the history of numerology, let us start using it!

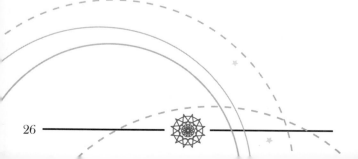

NUMBERS ARE THE UNIVERSAL LANGUAGE OFFERED BY THE DEITY TO HUMANS AS CONFIRMATION OF THE TRUTH.

ST AUGUSTINE OF HIPPO

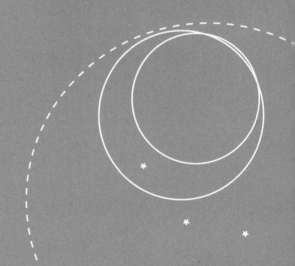

CHAPTER THREE:

NUMEROLOGY FOR SELF-DISCOVERY

As so many cultures across the world have discovered, numbers play a vital role in understanding our personalities, desires and destinies, and they can help us map out our journey through life. In this chapter, we will look at what makes up a numerology profile, breaking down each of the six core numbers and learning how to calculate each one. There is also guidance on each one's definition, meaning you can build and understand your profile and the profiles of others. So, grab your calculator and let's get started.

CREATING A
★ NUMEROLOGY PROFILE ★

A numerology profile is a sequence of numbers derived from your birth date and name, which can act as a personalized guide to your life. Your profile reveals key parts of your personality, including your strengths, weaknesses, goals, desires, first impressions and important characteristics. Much like an astrological natal chart, a numerology profile can show who you are and may become. Like a sun sign or rising sign revealing a person's identity, each number in a profile tells a story.

Numerology profiles can be simple or complex, depending on how deeply you wish to explore them. In this book, we will analyze the six core numbers that make up your numerology profile: the soul, personality, destiny, birthday, life path and attitude numbers. Three numbers are derived from your name and three come from your date of birth. We will go over numerology profiles in this chapter, but here is a quick introduction.

Here's a brief explanation of what your core numbers represent:

1. **Soul Number:** Your inner desires and what fulfils your soul.
2. **Personality Number:** How other people see you (friends, family, co-workers).
3. **Destiny Number:** Where you are heading in life, who you'll ultimately become. It also represents the strengths you'll develop.
4. **Birthday Number:** The gifts with which you were born, your natural talents.
5. **Life Path Number:** The journey you are taking in life. It is your identity. Unlike the destiny number, which represents the person you are "destined" to be, the life path number represents "you" in all areas of life.
6. **Attitude Number:** Your attitude toward life and the first impression you give off.

These numbers can help you understand who you are, but the most significant is your life path number. This number is similar to your sun sign in astrology: it acts as your representative and guides you through life.

By learning to create a numerology profile, you can gain insight into yourself and the people in your life. Unlike an astrology chart that requires detailed knowledge of birth times and location, all you need is a name and a date.

✶ NAME NUMBERS ✶

Our name is one of the first things we receive, and it stays with us throughout our lives. It is our introduction, identity and legacy. It is so important that the first three numbers of our numerology chart (soul, personality and destiny) come from the secret numbers hidden within the letters of our names. By decoding them, we can unlock our power, discover how others see us and realize our heart's desires.

So, how do we turn letters into numbers? No, there are no magic spells or tricky calculations required. Instead, we look to our old friend, Pythagoras. Pythagoras didn't just provide the blueprint for numerology: he also gave us a number system that assigns a single-digit number to each letter of the alphabet, meaning A is 1, B is 2 and so on. We've provided a handy chart to guide you through this chapter.

★ PYTHAGOREAN NUMBER SYSTEM ★

Use this chart to break down the letters of your name when decoding your soul, personality and destiny number. You can use whatever name you identify with.

1	2	3	4	5	6	7	8	9
A	B	C	D	E	F	G	H	I
J	K	L	M	N	O	P	Q	R
S	T	U	V	W	X	Y	Z	

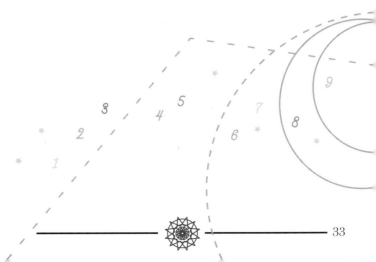

✦ HELPFUL NOTES ✦

Before we dive into the numbers in your numerology profile, it's important to bear these notes in mind.

SOMETIMES Y

When calculating your soul and personality numbers, vowels and consonants will be particularly important. But what if you have a Y in your name? Luckily, there is an easy trick to save you hours of headaches:

- If the Y is next to a vowel, it is a consonant. Examples include Bryan, Zoey and Greyson.
- If the Y is next to a consonant on BOTH sides, it is considered a vowel. Examples include Evelyn, Skylar and Dylan.

MASTER NUMBERS

Master numbers only stay intact when calculating life path numbers. If they appear in any other position, add them down to a single-digit number: 11 turns to 2; 22 turns to 4; 33 turns to 6. However, they will be more intense in this position. For example, if you have an 11 destiny number, you may have extra challenges and a deeper desire to achieve your goals.

⭐ SOUL NUMBER ⭐

The soul number comes first in your numerology profile, but it is the second most important. Our soul number tells us what we want most in this life – for what our soul hungers – and helps us identify the source of our deepest happiness. It essentially represents what we want, how we go after what we want and who we are at our core.

We obtain our soul number by adding all the vowels of our name together. For example, to get the soul number for **Elsie Wild**, we highlight all the vowels:

ELSIE WILD

$$5+9+5+9=28$$
$$2+8=10$$
$$1+0=1$$

Elsie Wild's soul number is 1.

★ SOUL NUMBER DEFINITIONS ★

Now that we have calculated Elsie's soul number, let's see what it means. Use the following pages to help you interpret your soul number.

1 Your soul craves success. You constantly strive for achievement and triumph – especially if the odds are against you. As an independent soul, you have the drive, determination and passion to go after what you desire. Your boldness and courage make you a natural leader, but your high standards make it difficult for you to ever find satisfaction.

2 Your soul needs to be surrounded by the people you love. You strive for balance, peace and harmony as you try to make everyone happy, even at a great personal cost. You have a big heart and unlimited patience, compassion and empathy. You find happiness in performing generous acts of kindness, but don't forget to request that same love in return.

3 Your soul needs to create. You have the heart of an artist with a deep desire to make. Whether you are a writer, musician, stylist or chef, you want to bring joy into people's lives. You are imaginative and outgoing. Believe in your dreams, but stay grounded.

4 Your soul aches for security and safety. Your soul is a planner. You need a back-up plan for your back-up plan to feel at ease. You are a diligent worker, grounded and organized. While you strive for structure and perfection, don't be afraid to have a little faith that things will work out.

5 Your soul desires freedom more than anything else. With the heart of an adventurer, you push past boundaries and limitations to discover something new and wonderful. You are curious, enthusiastic and the life of every party. You crave change and originality.

6 Your soul desires a home: the place where all your loved ones are. A natural caretaker, you are supportive, compassionate and empathetic. You need to feel helpful to feel good, even though you sometimes play the martyr.

7 Your soul desires to learn everything it can. From reading books to going on a spiritual journey, you hope to unlock the mysteries of the world. You are introspective and highly observant. You're happiest when alone in nature.

8 Your soul craves abundance. From financial independence to power and influence, you are ambitious and emotionally strong and have authoritative energy felt by all. Make sure your heart stays generous when you reach the success you seek.

9 You want to make the world a better place. You would do anything to help someone in need, from helping a friend in crisis to giving the last of your change to a stranger. Your soul heals when you let go of old familiar pains.

✶ PERSONALITY NUMBER ✶

After the soul number comes the personality number. While the soul number indicates your deepest desires and inner self, the personality number reveals your outer self: your public persona. Your personality number reveals how other people perceive you and can function as the mask you wear to the world. It shows up in your outer reactions, behaviours and how you carry yourself without being conscious of it.

We obtain our personality number by adding the consonants of our names together to get a single-digit number. For example, to get the personality number for Elsie Wild, we would highlight all the consonants.

ELSIE WILD

$$3+1+5+3+4=16$$
$$1+6=7$$

Elsie Wild's personality number is 7.

PERSONALITY ★ **NUMBER DEFINITIONS** ★

Now that we can calculate our personality number, let's see what the results mean.

1 People see you as a strong leader: independent and in control. Whether starting trends, leading on projects or setting up a business, people follow you. You are described as capable and determined, but can be seen as unreceptive and domineering.

2 People see you as a friendly person. Your modest nature makes you an excellent listener. You appear diplomatic, preferring to compromise than give an opinion. People describe you as friendly and understanding, but they may also say you are sensitive and a pushover.

3 You appear to have star quality. People assume you are an artist: a creator who wishes to inspire. People describe you as extroverted, optimistic and chatty. However, they may also say you can be exaggerating, moody and scattered.

4 You come across as someone who gets things done. Highly efficient and serious, people trust your decisions because you seem rational and knowledgeable. People describe you as dependable and trustworthy, but they may also say you can be predictable and stern.

5 You appear as someone who knows how to have fun. Passionate and ready for your next adventure. You always have a story to tell, from your latest escapade to the hottest gossip. People describe you as energetic and a free spirit, but they can also tell you're easily bored.

6 You tend to be a shoulder to cry on. Strangers pour their hearts out to you just because you said "hello" to them. You intuitively give people what they need. Often described as compassionate and nurturing, you can also come off as resentful and people-pleasing.

7 You come off as mysterious. An introvert, you seem lost in your own world, though you do open up when approached. People describe you as intelligent, private and observant. However, they may also call you arrogant and unfeeling.

8 Others see you as the boss. You walk with confidence and authority and are usually well-dressed. People sense your strong work ethic and know the lengths you'll go to achieve what you desire. Often described as ambitious and strong, though some call you intimidating.

9 You appear to be someone people can trust and have everyone's best interest at heart. You inspire people to be their best selves. People describe you as charismatic, spiritual and creative. However, you can come off as intimidating and envy-inducing.

IF YOU ONLY KNEW THE
MAGNIFICENCE OF THE
3, 6 AND 9, THEN YOU
WOULD HAVE A KEY
TO THE UNIVERSE.

NIKOLA TESLA

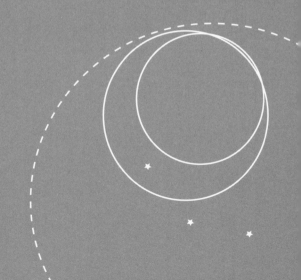

✦ DESTINY NUMBER ✦

While the life path number tells you about the journey you will take through life, the destiny number can reveal the end goal. This number shows the goals you will create for yourself in your family and work life and the legacy you wish to leave behind. If your destiny number and life path number are the same, it will be easy for you to achieve your goal. If they are different, it may take a longer time to reach your destiny.

Your destiny number is easy to calculate. Simply add your soul number and your personality number together. Let's try this with Elsie Wild.

Elsie Wild's soul number is 1,
and her personality number is 7.

$$1+7=8$$

Elsie Wild's destiny number is 8.

✦ DESTINY NUMBER DEFINITIONS ✦

Now that we calculated our number, let's see where our destiny lies.

1 A natural leader, your strength comes from your ability to accomplish remarkable things, thanks to your determination and drive. You have a long list of ambitions you wish to achieve during your time in this world. Your destiny is to become the best at what you do.

2 You have the gift of loving with no conditions, and it helps you bring out the best in everyone. You are graced with charm and a generous heart. Your destiny is to help create a better world, even if it is just making your world peaceful and loving.

3 A natural performer, your talents and strengths come from your creative mind, quick tongue and ability to make anything fun. However, while you love to hear the applause, your concern lies with hyping people up. Your destiny in life is to figure out how to bring joy to others.

4   Resolute and dependable, your strength is being able to manage any situation. You think rationally under stress. Your strong work ethic helps you achieve your dreams at a steady speed. Your destiny is to become an expert in your chosen field and share your knowledge.

5   You have the heart of an explorer, and your strength comes from your ability to take risks. You are gifted with a courageous spirit that makes you crave the variety of life. You are constantly on the move, celebrating life in all its glory. Your destiny is to experience everything you can.

6   You have the gift of making people feel loved and safe. Your natural aura of authority attracts people to you. Responsible, mature and deeply loyal, you are skilled at caring for others – from family members to clients. Your destiny is to build a solid, stable foundation.

7 An intellectual and quiet number, your strength lies in your power of observation. Using logic and intuition, you have the focus and interest to study anything. You work steadfastly toward your goals. Your destiny is to share your wisdom with the world.

8 Strong, determined and incredibly ambitious, you are a natural leader whose strength comes from your influence on others. Your desire for financial security and to achieve things drives you. Your destiny is to be an authority figure in your chosen field.

9 Your strength comes from your deep desire to make the world a better place. Your vision and ideas can win over almost anyone to your cause. Your compassionate and charitable heart can lead you to a higher state of consciousness. Your destiny is to use your unique qualities to help humanity.

⋆ BIRTH NUMBERS ⋆

After the name numbers, three numbers come from your birth day: your birthday number, life path and attitude number. Unlike the changeable name numbers, these are permanent and a key part of unlocking the secrets of your life.

⋆ BIRTHDAY NUMBER ⋆

The day you were born holds a great deal of influence on your life. This date was picked for you for a reason: to guide you on your higher purpose.

Your birthday number should be a single digit. If you were born on the first to the ninth of the month, this is your birthday number. If not, add the digits of your birthday to form a single-digit number. For example, if you were born on the seventh, your birthday number is 7. If you were born on the twenty-third, the number is 5 (2+3=5). If you were born on the twenty-ninth, your number is 2 (2+9=11, then 1+1=2).

✦ BIRTHDAY NUMBER DEFINITIONS ✦

Now that you calculated your birthday number, let's check its meaning.

1 If you were born on the first, tenth, nineteenth or twenty-eighth, you are skilled at taking the initiative. A self-starter, your strengths lie in your determination to succeed. You create your own opportunities, but you can be stubborn and selfish. Your lesson is to learn to share.

2 If you were born on the second, eleventh, twentieth or twenty-ninth, you are skilled at seeing all sides of a situation. This unbiased nature helps you find solutions for everyone. Your considerate and supportive nature means you work well in groups. Your strong intuition is your best gift, but you can be overly sensitive. Your lesson is to learn to stand up for yourself.

Note: If you were born on the eleventh, you have extremely high intuition: many people born on the eleventh are empaths or psychics.

3 If you were born on the third, twelfth, twenty-first or thirtieth, you are blessed with the gift of the gab. Your talent is creativity, making everything from art to positive vibes. Your strength is in your radiant joy and charisma. However, you have trouble with moodiness and lack direction. Your lesson is to learn to manage your big feelings.

4 If you were born on the fourth, thirteenth, twenty-second or thirty-first, you have a strong work ethic that allows you to persevere. You always have a plan and are organized, practical and good with details. While you're good at managing people, you have a difficult time relating to them with your blunt and inflexible nature. Your life's lesson is to learn that you don't need to control everything.

Note: If you were born on the twenty-second, you can achieve major things in your lifetime.

5 If you were born on the fifth, fourteenth or twenty-third, you are gifted with a quick wit. Your strength is your flexibility, love of change and adventurous spirit. However, you can be restless and easily bored. Your life's lesson is learning to finish what you started.

6 If you were born on the sixth, fifteenth or twenty-fourth, you are a nurturer. Your strength lies in your ability to heal people. You are loyal and have great instincts, but you can be meddlesome and play the martyr. Your life's lesson is to set boundaries to protect yourself.

7 If you were born on the seventh, sixteenth or twenty-fifth, you are blessed with an inquisitive mind. Your strengths lie in your intelligence and spiritual awareness. However, you are deeply private and need solitude to decompress. Your lesson is to balance private time and social relationships.

8 If you were born on the eighth, seventeenth or twenty-sixth, you are a success story in the making. Blessed with diligence and self-sufficiency, you have a talent for creating achievable goals. While you have a vast amount of personal power, you are accident-prone and need to remember to take care of your health. Your life's lesson is to learn that spiritual success is greater than material success.

9 If you were born on the ninth, eighteenth or twenty-seventh, you are a true humanitarian, working hard for the greater good. Blessed with a generous heart and an open mind, you have a talent for speaking up for others and find satisfaction in being of service. You don't seek leadership positions, but you exude so much confidence that people often put you in such roles. However, you can come off as condescending and distant. Your life's lesson is to forgive others.

NUMBERS RULE
THE UNIVERSE.

PYTHAGORAS

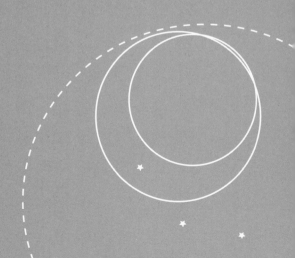

⭑ LIFE PATH NUMBER ⭑

Your life path number is the most important one in your numerology profile. It indicates who you are at your core and who you are meant to become. It shows you the path your life will take, so knowing it can help you navigate the journey. It can reveal the highs and lows of life and your strengths and weaknesses. Out of all the numbers in your profile, you will feel most connected to this one thanks to its guiding influence.

We calculate our life path number by adding our birthday numbers until we get to a single-digit number (unless you have a master number).

For example, if your birthday is 23 August 1994, you would add 2 and 3 (the day) to 8 (as August is the eighth month), plus the numbers in 1994, as shown here:

$$2+3+8+1+9+9+4=36$$
$$3+6=9$$

The life path number here is 9.

★ LIFE PATH NUMBER DEFINITIONS ★

Now that we calculated our life path numbers, let's see where they lead.

1   The number 1 is a straight line, standing alone and striving to reach the top. This describes the core of a 1 life path: an independent individual with a burning desire to win. What they win isn't important; the act of achieving goals and beating the competition is what gives them the real thrill. However, it can be lonely at the top.

Those with a 1 life path are born leaders: self-motivated, confident and filled with innovative ideas. They feel their best when in charge, working hard to succeed in all their goals and ambitions.

However, their competitive nature can be a double-edged sword. It pushes them toward success but can make them aggressive, domineering and self-centred, especially when they're not achieving fast enough. The biggest lesson is to be kinder to themselves and ask for help when needed.

2 The shape of the number 2 is curved, going in and out, showing the balance that a 2 life path number so deeply desires. Those with a 2 life path number seek harmony in every aspect of their lives and often bend over backward to get it.

A 2 life path number wishes to love and to be loved in return. It's not hard to love a 2 life path: they're kind, patient, easy-going and completely lovable. These traits come in handy when mediating conflicts or working as a team, as 2s hate to be alone. However, their greatest gift is their intuition guiding them through all situations.

One of 2's defining characteristics is emotion, which is a blessing and a curse. While their hypersensitivity gives them great compassion, feeling everyone's emotions can quickly drain their energy. A 2 life path number's biggest lesson is to balance their need to make everyone happy, including themselves.

3 Western numerology considers this number the luckiest because it looks like a pair of sideways horseshoes. This accounts for a 3 life path's incredible luck. Blessed with natural joie de vivre, these individuals shine like the stars they are, trying to lift spirits and bring joy to the world.

A 3 life path number is one of the most creative numbers in numerology – and the most talkative. These social creatures can connect with anyone using their clever humour, charisma and radiant optimism to attract and keep people's attention. People with a 3 life path number are natural performers and act like they are the main character in the story of their lives.

However, that isn't to say a 3 life path is perfect. They can easily become moody when their feelings are hurt. Their quick wit can bring a sharp tongue aimed at others and themselves. A 3's life purpose is to use their gift of communication to make the world a better place.

4 The number 4 looks like a carefully built number that consists of only straight, angular lines. This design fits perfectly with a 4 life path's need for order, efficacy and a stable foundation. A 4 does not leave things incomplete. A hard worker, 4 is here to finish a task and make sure it's built to last.

A 4 life path number takes a no-nonsense approach to life. They are the planners; if they're going to do something, they will do it right. Down-to-earth, rational and intelligent, these individuals devour information and enjoy sharing that knowledge. They are honest and expect honesty in return.

While 4 is sensible, they are not very flexible. They are often stubborn about their habits and opinions and rarely change because they fear the chaos that comes with uncertainty. Their life lesson is to learn how to take risks: it's the only way they'll grow.

5 The number 5 has an interesting shape. It opens at both the right and left and curves at the bottom. Its shape represents a 5's need for change, which they know is a consistent thing in life.

A 5 life path craves adventure. Even if they aren't the type to travel to far-off places or pull daredevil stunts, they'll happily read about it or create their own world of fun and escape; they are natural storytellers. Charming, enthusiastic and up for anything, 5s like to do things their way and live life to the fullest.

While they have a wide array of interests, they get easily bored and rarely finish what they start, preferring to move on to something new. They may even leave their comfort zone simply because they're bored. A 5 seeks to create a life from which they don't feel the need to escape.

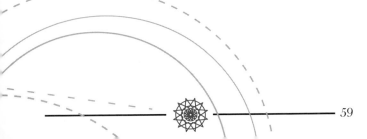

6   This number is often referred to as the "parent" of numerology, partly because its shape looks like a pregnant person. However, don't restrict 6 life paths to parenthood. They are people who give birth to ideas, art and the love they freely give to the world.

A 6 life path has a magnetic aura that welcomes people into their inner circle. Generous, loyal and nurturing, 6s often take in strays – from animals to people. They are not just a shoulder for people to cry on: they are willing to put in the time and effort to help solve people's problems, making them excellent friends.

While 6 is willing to do anything for someone, they can also overstep other people's boundaries and meddle in situations that don't involve them, voicing their strong opinions loudly. The life lesson for a 6 is learning to balance their sense of responsibility.

7 The number 7's curious shape means it looks similar to a boomerang. The similarity, however, is accurate because, much like a boomerang, a 7 life path will often go back to a subject, location or relationship, reflecting on how they can learn from it.

The scholar of numerology, a 7 life path is studious with an insatiable curiosity. You will often find them doing research and analysis just for fun. Analytical and inquisitive, 7s often try to balance their logical minds with their spiritual nature as they uncover the secrets of the universe.

While a 7 loves to discover other people's secrets, they keep their own private life heavily guarded. This gives them a reputation of being a loner, unable to connect with others as they wade into their research and view the world with a cynical eye. The lesson that a 7 life path must learn is to have faith – in themselves and others.

8 The number 8 is very powerful in numerology because it's shaped like a vertical infinity symbol. The infinity symbol contains the highs and lows of life, accurately showing the journey an 8 life path must go through. To get the best of what life has to offer, they will have to experience hardship.

People with an 8 life path are born influencers. They were meant to be successful, and though it will not come easy, they are willing to work for it. Assertive, powerful and resilient, they're not afraid to go on the rollercoaster of life as long as it leads to success.

However, 8 does not wish to be successful for the sake of it. They want the financial security and power that comes with achieving things. If their life is driven by money, they can become greedy, selfish and controlling. An 8 life path must learn that money and power are not the only markers of success.

9 Known as the number of completion, 9 is the most evolved in numerology, containing qualities of all the other numbers. It is shaped like a head full of wisdom from all the numbers. This wisdom means a 9 life path is here to guide others through life.

A 9 life path is an old soul. Humanitarians and idealists, their compassion, intelligence and moral compass guide their lives as they strive to make the world a better place. They also have a wicked sense of humour, a love for laughter and deep creativity. All things that they use to help others.

However, because 9s love to help others, they often come across as condescending martyrs, taking on the world's pain when no one asked them to. They also dig at old wounds from the past, never allowing themselves to heal. A 9's life lesson is to learn to let the past go and move on.

11 Being a master number, an 11 life path has more gifts than the average number. They also have more intense challenges they need to overcome. It is the most intuitive life path number in astrology, a gift that brings both rewards and drawbacks.

A person with a life path number of 11 is often considered ahead of their time. Blessed with two 1s, they have a pioneering spirit and a vision for revolutionary ideas. However, they have a tough time getting people on board and shelve their thoughts in favour of what best suits the group. They are creative, diplomatic and deeply sensitive. It is these traits that can help them be an inspiration to the world.

An 11 life path needs to learn to speak up for themselves. Highly self-critical and sensitive, they can easily talk themselves out of things. Their mission in life is to use their unique gifts to change the world – even if they do not see the rewards of their efforts.

22 Being a master number, a 22 life path has an intense journey through life. While they have much more to overcome to achieve their destiny, they also have the gifts to do so. For a 22, that gift is the ability to turn their visions into reality.

In numerology, 22 is known as the creator thanks to their rational nature taking dreams and turning them into achievable goals. However, they will have to work slowly and tirelessly over the years to bring their vision to life. Patience is required, but they have an abundance of that. Hardworking, diligent and knowledgeable, 22 can achieve great things.

People with a life path number of 22 often try to do everything on their own, having very little faith that someone else can do the job. This "I can do it myself" attitude can be isolating. The lesson for people with a 22 life path number is to create a legacy they can leave behind, but they need help to achieve that.

33 Those with a 33 life path number will not suffer the same hardships and challenges as other master numbers thanks to their two 3s making them a little luckier. A 33 life path is known as "The Deliverer" and is here to share their knowledge and ideas with the world.

Influential, compassionate and deeply creative, a 33 life path can communicate a clear message that is relatable to all. Whether through art, media or the power of speech, they will get their message across. They hope to use their gift to help the world and spread the message of healing.

However, 33s must heal themselves first. They have strong emotions that can lead them to act out of hurt, anger or jealousy. They will need to learn to be responsible for their actions. A 33's life path lesson is to learn to put their emotions aside to get their message across.

★ ATTITUDE NUMBER ★

The final number in your numerology profile is the attitude number. This number represents your attitude toward life and how you approach the world. It is also the very first impression you give off. Knowing your attitude number helps you understand how you see the world and how the world first sees you. It can also help you discover some of your natural abilities.

To find your attitude number, add your birth date and birth month together. Let's use Elsie Wild's dates as an example:

> Elsie Wild was born on 6 July,
> so you would add:
>
> 6+7=13
> 1+3=4

Elsie's attitude number is 4.

★ ATTITUDE NUMBER DEFINITIONS ★

Now let's take a look at your attitude number.

1 You have a winning attitude. Self-reliant and driven, you come across as someone who strives to achieve greatness in all aspects of life. You rarely ask for help, which can make you seem standoffish and competitive. You shine when receiving praise.

2 You have a pleasant attitude that makes you instantly likeable. Kind and highly perceptive to the energies and actions around you. This is often the number placement of psychics or people who see the world through a spiritual lens. However, you can be quite timid and shy.

3 You have the attitude of an artist and often find ways to express yourself creatively. You see the world through an optimistic lens that you wish to share. Despite being a social butterfly, you need a break from being "on" all the time, or people can see you being childish and a flake.

4 You have the attitude of dependability. Down-to-earth and logical, you approach life with a detailed plan, along with a back-up. However, you can come across as a worrier, constantly fretting over what cannot be controlled and overbearing about your concerns.

5 You have a fun-loving attitude. A free thinker, people often view you as a genius because of all of your innovative ideas. You view life as an adventure and embrace change. However, you can come off as reckless and immature.

6 You have the attitude of someone who loves to make social connections. To you, family isn't solely determined by blood. You consider your friends, pets, neighbours and employees as family. Like the head of the family, you can be a little overbearing and meddling, but you're the one people call in a crisis.

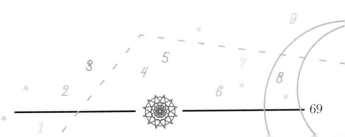

7 Your attitude is scholarly, and you are often found reading a book or observing other people. You give off a mysterious aura that makes you difficult to read. However, you are a great problem-solver, can see the details that others miss and analyze situations well.

8 You have an attitude of someone with power and influence. People are naturally intimidated by your strong aura, confidence and ambition that cannot be contained. You are often well dressed and although your motto is "fake it till you make it", you can be seen as cold.

9 You have the attitude of an activist. You see injustices and wish to fix them. Compassionate and socially conscious, you strive to help people and make the world a better place. While you can come off as self-righteous, you often give everything you have to your cause.

★ PUTTING IT ALL TOGETHER ★

Now that we've gone through every number in your numerology profile, take a look at this sample profile to see how it all comes together. This can help you make your own profile or one for your friends and family.

Let's say we are doing a numerology profile for someone named Avery Harris, who was born on 27 October 1998.

Avery Harris
27/10/1998

First, we calculate her soul number by adding all the vowels together:

AV**E**RY H**A**RR**I**S
1+5+1+9=16
1+6=7

Avery's soul number is 7.

Next, we calculate her personality number by adding all the consonants together:

AVERY HARRIS
4+9+7+8+9+9+1=47
4+7=11
1+1=2

Avery's personality number is 2.

Next, we have the destiny number, which we get by adding the soul and personality numbers together:

7+2=9

Avery's destiny number is 9.

Now the name numbers are done, we can move on to birth numbers, starting with the birthday number. Avery was born on the twenty-seventh:

2+7=9

Avery's birthday number is 9.

Then, the most important number, Avery's life path number:

27/10/1998
2+7+1+0+1+9+9+8=37
3+7=10
1+0=1

Avery's life path number is 1.

Finally, we have the attitude number:

27/10
2+7+1+0=10
1+0=1

Avery's attitude number is 1.

When we put all of those numbers together, we generate our numerology profile number:

Avery Harris
27/10/1998
Numerology profile: **72991/1**

Note that the attitude number is separated from the others with a "/". This is because it represents our attitude toward the outside world. Therefore, it is "outside" of the profile.

And there it is! Your whole numerology profile in just six simple steps. Now that you have this knowledge about the numbers that make you, *you*, you can use numerology to help take care of yourself.

CHAPTER FOUR:

NUMEROLOGY FOR SELF-CARE

Learning our numerology profile, especially our life path number, helps us understand who we are and how we can best look after ourselves. Each life path handles emotions differently, but they all require care. By learning the best ways to do so, you'll manage emotions and avoid getting lost in your struggles. Self-care is the maintenance that helps achieve your destiny.

In this chapter, we will discuss certain difficulties you may face according to your life path number and ways you can best nurture and care for yourself.

So, let's get started.

SELF-CARE ACCORDING TO YOUR LIFE PATH NUMBER

Match your life path number to the following definitions. Feel free to read about the other numbers in your chart, especially if it has repeating numbers, as they also have a major influence on your life.

1 As a fiercely competitive number, the only opponent they really have to face is themselves. Though they come off as confident, they are often consumed with self-doubt, especially when they don't receive the praise they crave. They can be hard on themselves, becoming their own worst enemies. A 1 life path number needs to learn to be kinder to themselves and find an outlet for their competitive streak to ensure they don't pick fights with others or themselves.

Self-Care Activities for a 1 Life Path:
Dancing, yoga, competitive sports, exercising, massage therapy, guided visualizations, positive affirmations.

Positive Affirmations for a 1 Life Path:
"Everything I need to succeed is within me."
"What is meant for me cannot miss me."
"I am worthy of what I desire."

2 As one of the most intuitive numbers in numerology, empathy can be both a 2 life path's biggest blessing and a major problem. This sensitivity can create extreme emotions in their lives that make them overjoyed one moment and leave them in tears the next. Being an empath can be draining as they sense everyone's feelings. The diplomat of numerology, they often sacrifice their feelings to make everyone happy – often at their own expense. This sensitivity can make them resentful and anxious. A 2 life path needs to develop healthy emotional boundaries to protect themselves.

Self-Care Activities for a 2 Life Path:
Music, tarot, journalling, photography, painting, knitting, swimming, meditating.

Positive Affirmations for a 2 Life Path:
"My feelings are as valid as everyone else's."
"It is not my job to manage everyone's emotions."
"I choose to nurture myself."

3 As the optimistic entertainer, a 3 life path is always "on", making jokes, telling a story, dressing up, putting on a performance. They wear a mask in front of the world, hiding their pain and hurt: they feel rejection to the core and often don't get over it for a long time. While they crave the spotlight, the moment the applause stops, their insecurity comes out. Their big emotions mean they can feel everything to extremes. They need to connect, understand and take responsibility for these emotions rather than have them take over the show or hide them away.

Self-Care Activities for a 3 Life Path:
Writing, painting, colouring, playing music, organizing their workspace, creating "to-do" lists, spending time alone.

Positive Affirmations for a 3 Life Path:
"I use my creative powers to stay centred and focused."
"I uplift and inspire people with my words."
"I'm creating a life that brings me joy."

4 A 4 life path is built around the need to feel safe and secure. However, this can make them rigid and unable to take risks or show vulnerability. A 4 life path can be somewhat pessimistic, noticing the flaws in the world and planning for the worst. They need to learn to move past the limits their negative mindset has created and live a richer life, starting with healing the problematic relationships they may have. Once they let go of that pain, they can move on.

Self-Care Activities for a 4 Life Path:
Taking an in-person class (especially a dancing or cooking class), doing a puzzle, meditating, travelling, building something, reading.

Positive Affirmations for a 4 Life Path:
"I am open to new experiences."
"I am safe and secure."
"I am growing at my own pace."

5 A 5 life path number loves life but can get bored easily. While this approach makes their lives very exciting, it can also lead to a constant search for escapism. If they cannot find a healthy outlet that holds their focus, they can become self-destructive. Energetic and bold, they can get exhausted by burning the candle at both ends, taking on too many things at once. Life is an adventure – there's no need to rush! A 5 life path needs to learn to appreciate the joy life brings. Be present.

Self-Care Activities for a 5 Life Path:
Travelling, visiting friends, reading, watching movies, massages, having new experiences.

Positive Affirmations for a 5 Life Path:
"I am here in this moment, and I enjoy it."
"I have a life I don't need to escape from."
"Every choice is an opportunity for me to be my best self."

6 Those with a 6 life path number have a big heart, but it can sometimes be a little too big, and they can find it difficult to place boundaries. They'll easily invite those that are struggling into their home and nurse them back to health. However, when they take in the wrong kind of person, they can easily be manipulated, used and betrayed. On the other hand, 6 can easily insert themselves into other people's lives without being asked. Wanting to feel useful, they'll often take over; this can breed resentment on both sides. A 6 life path needs to nurture themselves more.

Self-Care Activities for a 6 Life Path:
Making a nice meal, decorating, making art, chatting with a friend, watching movies, hosting a family dinner.

Positive Affirmations for a 6 Life Path:
"I am open to creative solutions."
"I accept everyone has to live their own life."
"I am very loved."

7 The most serious number in numerology, 7's privacy makes them difficult to get to know. While this somewhat secretive attitude can help them thrive in certain situations, they often struggle with intimate social relationships and may choose to self-isolate out of fear of rejection. Instead of connecting, they get trapped in their own head, overthinking everything to the point of anxiety. However, a 7 can find peace, comfort and community in a spiritual base.

Self-Care Activities for a 7 Life Path:
Researching a new topic, going out in nature, astrology, tarot, warm baths, reading, travelling, meditation, writing in a gratitude journal.

Positive Affirmations for a 7 Life Path:
"I have faith that things will work out for the best."
"I am connected to my spiritual path."
"I know my own truth."

8 An 8's life can be a rollercoaster. On top of the world one moment, going down the next.

As a person who strives for power and success at all costs, the lows of life can be particularly tough. Accident-prone and quick-tempered, an 8 often rams their way through life and gets hurt in the process. An 8 needs to learn they can't control everything. That despite all their power and good work ethic, they can't get everything they want the moment they want it. Such knowledge can prevent drastic highs and lows.

Self-Care Activities for an 8 Life Path:
Breathwork, balancing your budget, taking regular breaks, painting, sewing, writing, baths, stretching.

Positive Affirmations for an 8 Life Path:
"I have all the resources I need."
"I am a powerful force. People respect me."
"The more I have, the more I can share."

9   As the humanitarian of numerology, 9 life paths are experts at taking care of other people and being of service to their loved ones or even strangers. However, because they create such a confident, unflappable impression, no one notices when they need help. While everyone assumes they are well, they could, in fact, be suffering, not knowing how to ask for help. They are not easy to read. They should vocalize what they need and be willing to ask for it, even if they don't want to.

Self-Care Activities for a 9 Life Path:
Meaningful conversations, meditating, yoga, fiction writing, watercolour painting, volunteering, journalling, hiking.

Positive Affirmations for a 9 Life Path:
"I deserve to have all of my needs met."
"I let go of the past and embrace my present."
"I trust that my path is leading me toward my highest good."

11 Being a master number, those with 11 life paths will face more challenges and obstacles throughout their lives than most others. Because of this, self-care is vital. Elevens are deeply sensitive in all areas of life, especially when it comes to criticism. Their life lesson is to take that criticism and learn from it, but the hurt words cause can leave deep scars. They need to remember their own truth, not someone else's.

Self-Care Activities for an 11 Life Path:
Tarot reading, dancing, art, writing, spending time with animals, sleeping under a weighted blanket.

Positive Affirmations for an 11 Life Path:
"I honour my feelings, but I don't let them control me."
"I am open to the messages that the universe has to offer me."
"Other people's opinions of me are none of my concern."

22 Another master number, those with a 22 life path number will find that making a dream a tangible reality will present higher hurdles and more roadblocks than usual. Life tends to bring 22s an abundance of problems to solve. While each problem delivers an important life lesson, it can also bring nervousness and anxiety. They will need to hone their patience and learn to become resilient and creative when going through life to achieve everything they desire.

Self-Care Activities for a 22 Life Path:
Mood boarding, woodworking, running, breathwork.

Positive Affirmations for a 22 Life Path:
"I release the fears that do not serve me."
"I strive for satisfaction, not for perfection."
"I deserve the opportunities and abundance I receive."

33 As a master number, a 33 faces unique challenges that differ from regular numbers, particularly when it comes to taking responsibility. In youth, a 33 life path will avoid responsibility whenever possible, focusing more on having fun. However, they cannot escape their responsibilities, which are often thrust onto them in dramatic and life-altering ways. Growing up is a ritual of extremes; in trying to keep their head above water, they may struggle to take care of their own emotional needs. A 33 must juggle healing their inner child while also trying to grow into a successful adult.

Self-Care Activities for a 33 Life Path:
Interior decorating, performing in front of a crowd, colouring, socializing with friends, writing in a planner, being pampered.

Positive Affirmations for a 33 Life Path:
"I am healing every day."
"I take responsibility for myself first."
"I am optimistic because today is brand new."

CRYSTALS FOR
★ EACH LIFE PATH NUMBER ★

Crystal healing can be a wonderful way for each life path number to heal, recharge and bring balance to their lives. And with so many crystal options in the world, you can find one to suit every need, from finding confidence to de-stressing.

There are numerous ways to use crystals in your life, from wearing them as jewellery, holding them while meditating and introducing them around your home, to placing them on your body to gain the healing powers that certain crystals can provide. Play around with your crystals and see what methods work best for you and your self-care needs.

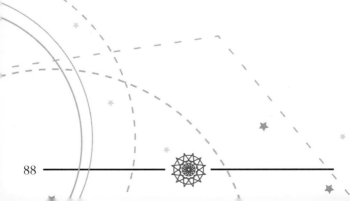

Here are some crystal recommendations based on each life path number's specific needs.

1 As an independent leader, 1 needs to remember that they are always worthy of a win, to remember what they are passionate about and to know when to remain calm and be a team player. Some crystals that would benefit a 1 are:

- **Citrine:** Citrine brings out the best in a 1 life path: confidence, individuality and resilience. It can also provide extra vitality, help realize goals and offer new insights.
- **Ruby:** Ruby is a powerful grounding stone that brings courage and strength. It encourages leadership qualities by strengthening decisiveness, motivation and alertness.
- **Sunstone:** Known as the stone of leadership, sunstone gives us the power to change our lives and open our hearts to helping others. Sunstone calms our worries and fears by bringing optimistic vibrations that everything will work out for the best.

2 and 11

As empaths, 2 and 11 life path numbers feel everything with intensity, so they'll need a crystal that can balance their emotions and fill them with positivity and light when they're drained. Some crystals that would benefit 2 and 11 are:

- **Aventurine:** An ideal stone for cleansing the aura and bringing a calming vibration to anyone wearing it. Aventurine can help relax the mind and provide the inner strength and stability that 2s and 11s need.
- **Moonstone:** Like 2s and 11s, moonstone is a natural harmonizer, balancing the mind, body and spirit into a steady, peaceful flow. It can also boost our natural intuition, especially when placed under a pillow before bed. Moonstones encourage us to be gentle and open to the positive energy of life.
- **Rose Quartz:** The perfect stone for 2 and 11 life paths, rose quartz is the stone of universal love. Rose quartz brings feelings of self-love, heals emotional wounds and protects us from negative influences.

3 Lucky number three, 3 life paths are bubbly, charming and always have a smile to give and joke to tell. However, they could use a crystal that can help them focus their attention to finish projects and something to keep their emotions in check. Some crystals that would benefit 3s are:

- **Blue Topaz:** A stone of happiness, blue topaz can help us identify our goals and find fulfilment. It has the power to banish any negative vibe or feeling and can promote self-healing.
- **Malachite:** Known as the stone of transformation, malachite helps bring our deepest desires to the surface and lets us become more aware of what we want. Malachite helps us make decisions and heal emotional pain.
- **Sodalite:** Those with a 3 life path can often get caught up in their own myths and stories. Sodalite can help calm their mind and encourage rational thought and truth-telling. It can also help connect them to their spiritual side.

4 and 22

Stable and dependable, 4 and 22 life path numbers are always busy planning. However, they can miss out on the excitement in life. They could use a stone that will encourage them to have a little more fun and flexibility. Some crystals that would benefit 4s and 22s are:

- **Aquamarine:** The stone of peace and clarity, aquamarine is the perfect cleansing gemstone, making the stressed 4s and 22s feel calm and stable. It can help end old cycles and start something new.
- **Garnet:** This fiery crystal can help bring passion to life and give 4s and 22s the bravery and boldness they need to achieve their dreams. Garnet offers a boost of self-confidence and protection to take calculated risks.
- **Labradorite:** The stone for those who overwork, labradorite can help bring energy back into the body while healing the spirit. One of the most powerful protection stones, labradorite can act as a shield to prevent negative energy and provide strength.

5 Bold, adventurous and freedom-loving, 5s constantly live life to the fullest. However, always looking for stimulation can drain 5s, especially if they don't take time to rest. A 5 life path needs to remember to take care of themselves and not burn out trying to keep the party going. Some crystals that would benefit 5s are:

- **Emerald:** Known as the crystal of divine inspiration, emerald generates unique ideas and opinions. Emerald also provides the wisdom and patience to make those ideas a reality. It can heal emotional pain, replacing it with peace and love.
- **Green Moss Agate:** Green moss agate provides the grounding influence the escapist 5 desperately needs. This crystal offers a balance of spiritual freedom and personal responsibility to help 5s feel happy without burning out.
- **Tiger's Eye:** A stone of good fortune, tiger's eye brings security, confidence and courage, motivating us to achieve our goals and desires.

6 and 33

As the caretakers of numerology, 6 and 33 life path numbers need to remember to care for themselves before they can tend to the entire world. They'll need crystals that can protect their big hearts, help them speak their truths and keep them from burning out. Some crystals that would benefit 6s and 33s are:

- **Amber:** A powerful healing stone, amber can help cleanse the negative energy that 6s and 33s tend to absorb from others, allowing their body, mind and spirit to heal. Amber can boost strength, success, joy and patience.
- **Morganite:** A stone to heal a broken heart and provide the courage to love ourselves the way we love others. Morganite brings relaxation and calming energy and removes the pressures we've placed on ourselves.
- **Unakite:** A regenerating crystal that can help heal family relationships and stabilize our personal energy. It can also help us show more assertiveness about what we need in life.

7   More than anything, 7s need help to embrace their spiritual side. Sceptics, by nature, have a tough time trusting anything they cannot see or prove with rational logic. They need crystals that can help increase their intuition, energize their spirit and help them on the path to enlightenment. Some crystals that would benefit 7s are:

- **Amethyst:** A natural tranquilizer, amethyst helps heal the stresses felt by 7s, especially when they are overthinking. This spiritual crystal provides wisdom and intuition and helps with divination. It can also provide emotional and mental protection.
- **Lapis Lazuli:** Known as the stone of enlightenment, lapis lazuli is a powerful stone that can help open the mind and strengthen our intellectual abilities.
- **Orange Calcite:** For cynical 7s, orange calcite can bring extra positivity and confidence into their lives. The crystal can also help improve memory, increase trust and help them organize their lives with steadfast energy.

8 Powerful and authoritative, 8s can sometimes get so wrapped up in their quest for influence, money and fame that it can be their downfall. They need crystals to keep them balanced and help them remember what's important in life. These accident-prone individuals can also profit from a protective crystal. Some crystals that would benefit 8s are:

- **Black Tourmaline:** One of the strongest protective crystals, black tourmaline can guard 8s against disloyalty, secret enemies and negativity. Black tourmaline can boost perseverance to bring abundance into our lives.
- **Rhodonite:** For the 8s that come off as cool and unforgiving, rhodonite can help open their hearts and bring reconciliation to even the worst conflicts. Rhodonite has a soothing effect that can help calm the soul.
- **Sapphire:** Considered to be the wisdom stone, sapphire can promote concentration, remove unwanted thoughts and help enchant our creative mind to find unique solutions. Sapphire can also prevent materialism and allow us to find abundance from within.

9 People with a 9 life path number can achieve anything they want, though sometimes they can act as their own worst enemies. They need crystals that prevent self-sabotage and boost self-confidence. They also need crystals that help them express their emotions constructively. Some crystals that would benefit 9s are:

- **Jasper:** The "mother of all crystals" can help ground the overthinking 9 and bring them courage, understanding and a boost of wisdom. Wearing jasper can help guide our intentions to do good work.
- **Peridot:** Peridot is the stone of compassion, bringing health, peace and a little luck to our lives. Peridot can also balance our emotions and mind, especially if dealing with feelings of guilt and hurt. Peridot encourages creativity and being social.
- **Smoky Quartz:** A stress-relieving crystal, smoky quartz brings emotional calmness and promotes positive thoughts and actions. It also helps raise spiritual awareness about using our gifts for the highest good.

CHAPTER FIVE:

NUMEROLOGY
FOR DIVINATION

Like astrology, tarot and tea reading, numerology can be used for divination and self-reflection. Numbers often send us secret messages from the universe, guiding us in the right direction, and they can help predict our futures.

Throughout this chapter, we will examine how numerology can help us see into the future, whether to explain why you've been seeing the number 2 everywhere or what the new year has in store for you. We will also cover how numerology affects other forms of divination, such as tarot.

So, grab your calculator and a crystal ball and let's see what the future has in store!

THE FUTURE DEPENDS ON WHAT WE DO IN THE PRESENT.

MAHATMA GANDHI

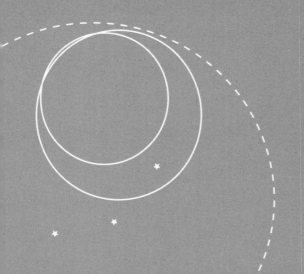

✦ ANGEL NUMBERS ✦

Have you ever seen a number pop up multiple times during a certain time frame? Those are the angel numbers, and they can have spiritual significance in your life. You might notice this number throughout your daily life or in your other divination practices, such as tarot, tea reading and crystal ball scrying.

For example, you might go shopping and realize your bill is £33.33, then go to work and get an important phone call at 3.33 p.m. You then do a tarot pull and get the 3 of wands, or maybe you find a trio of missed notifications on your phone. The number 3 is following you.

Whether you believe these messages are coming from your guardian angels, your spirit guide, the universe or even just your subconscious mind trying to give you a hint, repeating numbers are no coincidence. They show up for a specific reason.

✦ ANGEL NUMBER DEFINITIONS ✦

So, what is the universe trying to tell you? Let's take a look at angel numbers' meanings.

111

It's time to start manifesting. Seeing a sequence of 1s represents the beginning of a new chapter in your life. Now is the perfect time to create the life you want and make your desires a reality. The universe is telling you to keep your eyes peeled for opportunities and assuring you it's okay to take some calculated risks. It is an ideal time to start new projects, new relationships or just change your life for the better.

222

Love is all around you when you see a sequence of 2s. Whether you have just started dating, entered a relationship or even begun collaborating on a project, seeing 2s is the universe giving its support to your new partnerships. However, if you're still working solo, this is the universe telling you to team up with someone. You're going in the right direction, but don't do it alone.

333

Three is one of the luckiest numbers, and seeing it in a sequence is a positive sign from the universe that your prayers will be answered or your manifestation will soon come to life. This is an ideal time to trust your gut and go after what you want, from applying for your dream job to moving to a new city. You'll find that opportunities come easily and your needs are met. Don't overthink this. It's just spirit guides showing you that they have your back.

444

A sequence of 4s shows up in your life when you're going through a rough patch: you may be dealing with a difficult break-up, have received bad news or are just going through a period of loneliness, depression or anxiety. All may feel lost, but 4 reminds you that your spirit guides are close by, protecting you. Ground yourself, things won't be bad for much longer.

555

Get ready for some major changes in your life when you see a sequence of 5s. If things seem quiet, get ready, as some big shake-ups will happen soon. This is a sign of dramatic transformation that will affect many aspects of your life. Despite this period's intensity, 5 provides assurance that it is all for the best. This restructuring of your life is happening for your highest good, so embrace the chaos.

666

Don't freak out! Seeing 666 is NOT the sign of the devil. However, it IS a sign that your life has gotten seriously off-track. When you see a sequence of 6s, it's the universe telling you to get back to basics and out of your own way. This nurturing energy helps you become grounded to stop overthinking or overworking. Let go of what isn't serving you and move on!

777

While it is a very lucky thing to see on a slot machine or a scratch card, a sequence of 7s in real life is a sign to step up your spiritual game (and step out of the casinos). Your guides are telling you to focus on your spiritual journey, especially if you've lost your way recently. This shift in focus can occur in prayer, meditation, spell casting, getting into nature or helping others. Whatever may help you get on the path toward enlightenment.

888

A sequence of 8s symbolizes an incoming period of abundance. If you see 8s while working or dealing with money, it may represent a financial windfall or signify getting more clients and work opportunities. If you see these 8s while dating or with your partner, more love is on its way. Seeing 8s on the clock could mean more free time. Whatever it is, receive it with open arms.

999

The number 9 is the number of completion, so when you see a sequence of them, the universe is telling you that a chapter of your life is coming to a close. Whether you've just finished a job, graduated from school or have ended an important relationship, it's time to wrap things up. However, this isn't always a sad thing; when one cycle ends, another will soon begin. But you'll need to let go of this phase and trust the process, even if it's hard.

LESSER-KNOWN ANGEL NUMBERS

Angel numbers don't always have to repeat a single number. Seeing sequences of any combination of numbers over and over can be a secret code from the universe. Here are some to look out for.

- **1212:** You're about to change your mind about an important issue.
- **72:** A miracle is going to happen.
- **123**: Your efforts will soon pay off.

YOUR LIFE IS A STORY OF TRANSITION. YOU ARE ALWAYS LEAVING ONE CHAPTER BEHIND WHILE MOVING ON TO THE NEXT.

ANONYMOUS

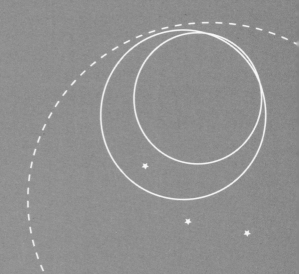

✴ PERSONAL YEAR NUMBER ✴

Life flows through a series of cycles, from the cycles of the seasons to the cycle of life. Numerology is also based on cycles, starting with 1, the number of creation and beginnings, to 9, the cycle of completion. In numerology, we consistently go through the nine phases that mark one chapter of our lives. This is known as the personal year number.

Our personal year number indicates what stage we are in, informs us what energy that year will have for us and tells us the theme of our year. By knowing our personal year number, we can not only anticipate what challenges, events and opportunities the year may have in store for us but can also make important decisions. By knowing what lies ahead, we can make the choices that best suit our lives.

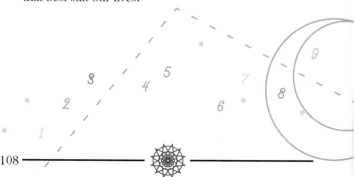

Finding your personal year number is simple. Just add your attitude number (birth month + birth day) to the year you wish to calculate. For example, if you want to know your personal year number for 2022 and your attitude number is 4, this is the method you use:

4+2+0+2+2=10
1+0=1

Your personal year number would be 1.

Go through these personal year numbers to better understand your current phase of life and what your year has in store for you.

Important Note: If your personal year is the same number as your life path number, you will feel the vibration of the year with greater intensity. It will be a time of immense success when you'll get everything you've been working toward, but it can create a new set of challenges, depending on that year's theme.

PERSONAL YEAR 1

This is a year of new and exciting beginnings. It is a new cycle where you can feel that energy in everything you do. Don't concern yourself with the past. That chapter of your life is over, and this slate is clean.

No pressure, but everything you do this year will influence the next nine years of your life. Intimidating, yes, but this year gives you the energy and confidence to take on the challenge. This is the year of planting seeds. Even tiny actions you may not think about now will have a great effect later, so make sure you do everything with purpose. Opportunities are everywhere, so seize them.

The negative aspect of this year is that it's not a great time to start a new relationship, as you'll be more focused on yourself. If you're single, focus on building a strong relationship with yourself and even change your image if you want. You are standing on your own and becoming independent. Embrace it.

PERSONAL YEAR 2

Life begins to calm down in a 2 year. After a year of action and independence, our lives start to settle, and we begin to put down roots and look for a little more peace. It is a year when we don't have to do everything alone.

This is a year for relationships of all kinds: friendships, romantic relationships, creative and business partnerships, or even just working as a collective. You don't have a lot of desire to be by yourself and will learn plenty of lessons regarding patience, cooperation and how to be a good teammate. Fortunately, it will be easy to get along with people this year.

The downside of this year is the ease of becoming co-dependent on another person, which is why balance is so key. Make sure there is give and take in your more important relationships and remember to spend plenty of time taking care of yourself.

PERSONAL YEAR 3

Get ready to have some fun because this is the year of creative success. This year, you will flow with creative energy, brilliant new ideas and hope for the future. This is a time for optimism, dreams and tons of fun.

You'll expand your social circle this year, meeting people from all walks of life. You'll listen to new ideas, debate exciting topics, change your mind and share your dreams. This is an ideal year to work on creative jobs, attend school or even get noticed by all the "right" people who can help you succeed.

Don't enter into any relationships that you don't truly want, especially if they are romantic. Falling in love is easy, but it's hard to stay committed to anything, be it a person, an idea or an occupation. You need the freedom to do what you want. It is very important not to limit yourself.

PERSONAL YEAR 4

You spent the last year forming ideas and opinions and exploring your options. Now is the time to pick something and stick to it. You're building a foundation for your life, so roll up your sleeves and get to work.

The most important thing this year is to establish security for yourself. This could mean deciding the next step in your education, finding a steady job that pays your bills or perhaps settling down with someone. This is a time of major decision-making, so make it count. You'll create plans to see you through the next few years, so focus your energy on a certain craft, project, relationship, job or dream. You'll be setting yourself in the direction that you need to go.

However, it can also be a year of stagnation, especially for those afraid to make decisions. It's easy to fall into ruts this year or to be so busy working and planning that you miss out on all the fun. Remember to take time out to enjoy life.

PERSONAL YEAR 5

After spending the entirety of last year making plans, the universe will let you know what plans are worth keeping by bringing sudden, dramatic changes into your life. This is a year of unexpected break-ups, job loss or major moves, and will remind you that change is the only sure thing.

So, don't waste time grieving over the future that "might have been". It wasn't meant for you, so move on! Instead, embrace your newfound freedom. This is a year of adventure and excitement. It's an ideal time to explore new opportunities, find new passions and allow yourself to grow. Keep an open mind, and you may discover the person you're meant to be.

However, you can be a little *too* carefree this year. If these changes are a lot for you, you may develop some pretty bad habits to cope with them. It's easy to be reckless and irresponsible, so look for ways to stay grounded and find healthy coping mechanisms.

PERSONAL YEAR 6

Things will fall back into a harmonious and peaceful place after last year. After taking some time to explore new roads and opinions, you will have new choices to make and new responsibilities.

Home and family will take on greater importance this year. You may start thinking about entering into a serious relationship or spending more time with your family. Or perhaps things like marriage, children or getting a home will become your priority. You may need to take care of relatives or your home that year.

Whatever the case may be, this year will see you taking on many new responsibilities. This can make you feel needed and important but also overwhelmed. This is both a joyful and stressful period, so remember to take care of yourself too, as it will be easy to ignore your health. Sacrificing your health now can lead to a crisis later.

PERSONAL YEAR 7

After a year of taking care of other people, 7 brings a year of introspection and soul-searching. This is a year of personal growth as you'll encounter some big truths that could affect your relationships, job and even how you think about yourself. You'll need your faith more than ever this year – even if it's just faith in yourself.

This year can manifest itself in diverse ways. Some people go back to school. Some travel by themselves, visiting new places or going on retreats. Some get into religion and spirituality and even start practising things like tarot, astrology and numerology (you may be reading this book in a 7 year). Intuition will increase this year, and you may even have psychic flashes. Trust them.

However, this can be a very lonely year as you won't want to spend time with many people. Relationships can end or become deeply strained. It's important to spend time in nature to heal and restore your faith.

PERSONAL YEAR 8

After a year of introspection, you're ready to step into your personal power. Last year you were the student; now, you're the expert. This is a karmic return: whatever you've been doing the last eight years will be rewarded, for better or worse.

This is a year of rewards in all forms. You may receive a financial reward in the form of a raise, an inheritance, a return on an investment, a new car or a new home. You may receive the reward of power: getting a promotion, becoming an influencer or being considered the "best" in your field. You may just receive a bunch of praise. Use your rewards wisely: this power can be a blessing and a test.

However, if you've made poor decisions over the last few years, you'll be paying for them now. Punishments will be doled out, gains become losses, and you may lose things that were important to you because you didn't earn them. The universe is balancing itself now.

PERSONAL YEAR 9

We're at the end of an era. This is the final year of your cycle and the ending of an important journey of your life. This can be a bittersweet period, especially if you are not ready to say goodbye to this phase of your life.

This is a year of tying up loose ends and getting ready to start the next chapter, even if you aren't aware of it. This is often a time of graduations, major milestones and just feeling more mature than you were nine years ago. You may find yourself more compassionate this year, doing volunteer work, spending time with loved ones or just reflecting on where you have been and where you want to go.

You'll be doing a lot of thinking this year, but perhaps refrain from starting anything new, especially relationships or businesses. Instead, focus on the wisdom you have gained and think about your next great adventure. One cycle is ending, but a new one is around the corner.

★ TAROT AND NUMEROLOGY ★

Tarot and numerology often go hand in hand in terms of understanding the importance of numbers. Knowing a lot about numerology makes it easier to understand tarot. And, in turn, if you understand tarot, learning numerology becomes easier.

Tarot is a form of divination that uses 78 specific cards divided into two groups: 22 cards (a master number) in the major arcana and 56 cards (5+6=11, another master number) in the minor arcana. All the cards are numbered, with the minor arcana divided into four sections labelled from 1 to 10.

If you're learning tarot for the first time, having a good understanding of numerology will only elevate the experience, as it gives you insights into the meaning of the cards and may even be the universe giving you a message.

Here's a quick guide to tarot cards and their corresponding numbers.

CARDS WITH A 1 VIBRATION

- **The Magician (1):** Represents willpower, manifestation, creation, skill, desire.
- **The Wheel of Fortune (10):** Represents destiny, fortune, success, luck.
- **The Sun (19):** Represents success, positivity, vitality, fun.
- **Ace (Ace of Wands, Cups, Swords, Pentacles):** Raw potential.

CARDS WITH A 2 VIBRATION

- **The High Priestess (2):** Represents intuition, spirituality, higher power, inner voice.
- **Justice (11):** Represents equality, truth, fairness, law.
- **Judgement (20):** Represents awakening, renewal, decisiveness, transformation.
- **2 (2 of Wands, Cups, Swords, Pentacles):** Duality.

CARDS WITH A 3 VIBRATION

- **The Empress (3):** Represents expression, creativity, beauty, nurturing.
- **The Hanged Man (12):** Represents waiting, sacrifice, perspective, lack of direction.
- **The World (21):** Represents completion, accomplishment, travel, new beginnings.
- **3 (3 of Wands, Cups, Swords, Pentacles):** Unity.

CARDS WITH A 4 VIBRATION

- **The Emperor (4):** Represents stability, reason, conviction, protection.
- **Death (13):** Represents endings, change, transformation, letting go.
- **4 (4 of Wands, Cups, Swords, Pentacles):** Stability.

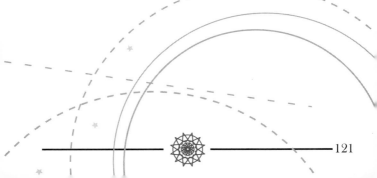

CARDS WITH A 5 VIBRATION

- **The Hierophant (5):** Represents tradition, social groups, knowledge, beliefs.
- **Temperance (14):** Represents economy, moderation, management, accommodation.
- **5 (5 of Wands, Cups, Swords, Pentacles):** Change.

CARDS WITH A 6 VIBRATION

- **The Lovers (6):** Represents commitment, partnerships, harmony, choices.
- **The Devil (15):** Represents temptation, attachment, restriction, obsession.
- **6 (6 of Wands, Cups, Swords, Pentacles):** Harmony.

CARDS WITH A 7 VIBRATION

- **The Chariot (7):** Represents success, control, self-discipline, ambition.
- **The Tower (16):** Represents sudden change, chaos, awakening, revelation.
- **7 (7 of Wands, Cups, Swords, Pentacles):** Higher purpose.

CARDS WITH AN 8 VIBRATION

- **Strength (8):** Represents power, action, courage, success.
- **The Star (17):** Represents hope, renewed power, strength, healing.
- **8 (8 of Wands, Cups, Swords, Pentacles):** Boundaries.

CARDS WITH A 9 VIBRATION

- **The Hermit (9):** Represents self-reflection, contemplation, solitude, learning.
- **The Moon (18):** Represents illusion, intuition, complexity, secrets.
- **9 (9 of Wands, Cups, Swords, Pentacles):** Completion.

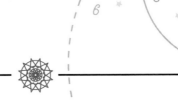

DIVINATION WITH DICE

While we see numbers everywhere, if you have a certain question or want a little guidance from the universe using numerology, all you need to do is roll the dice. Practising dice divination can give you a quick number answer to any question you may have.

To practise dice divination, you just need two six-sided dice. Hold them in your hand as you meditate on your question. Your question shouldn't be one that can be answered with a "yes" or "no". Instead, the questions should be more like, "What is the energy of the day?" or "What do I need right now?"

Then, when you are ready, shake the dice in your hands and roll them. What number did you get? Remember to add the number into a single digit. For example, if you roll a 2 and a 3, your answer is 5.

You can roll multiple times to get an angel number or just reflect on the vibration of your number as your answer. Use your intuition to guide you.

★ CONCLUSION ★

While we have reached the end of this book, this is just the beginning of your journey through numerology. Now you have the basics, you can go forward and learn more about yourself and the world around you. There is so much to gain from understanding how your numerology profile shows up in your personality and your journey through life. Now you know why you have a certain "lucky" number or why you're having a very busy year. You can even start performing number readings for your loved ones to better understand how they tick and further your relationships.

You can even use numerology to make more conscious decisions in your life. Maybe you will consider changing your name or using a new nickname to help with your ambitions, or you may even make different choices about what house you live in, just based on the street number. Remember, it's important not to get so hyper-focused on what the numbers mean that you forget about your own free will. Above all else, you hold your destiny in your hands.

So go forward, keep growing and learning. This is only the beginning.

★ RESOURCES ★

If you're interested in learning more about numerology, here are some resources to check out to help you continue your practice.

BOOKS

- Elffers, Joost and Goldschnider, Gary *The Secret Language of Relationships: Your Complete Personology Guide to Any Relationship with Anyone* (2013, Avery)
- McCants, Glynis *Glynis Has Your Number: Discover What Life Has in Store for You Through the Power of Numerology!* (2005, Hachette Book)
- Ngan, Nicholas David *Your Soul Contract Decoded: Discovering the Spiritual Map of Your Life with Numerology* (2013, Watkins)
- Woodward, Joy *A Beginner's Guide to Numerology: Decode Relationships, Maximize Opportunities, and Discover Your Destiny* (2019, Rockridge Press)

WEBSITES

- www.numerologist.com
- www.feliciabender.com
- www.creativenumerology.com